AIR FRYER

cookbook

Air Fryer Recipe Book: Quick and easy and effortless recipes to master the full potential of your oven. Boost metabolism and achieve rapid weight loss

TABLE OF CONTENTS

—

INTRODUCTION

The big day has arrived! You finally have your hands on your shiny new Air Fryer. But you're probably wondering what it is and how to get set up. No worries, this chapter is designed with beginners in mind. First, let's begin by talking about the Air Fryer in general. Simply put, an Air Fryer is a countertop convection oven that cooks food with hot air. This is great because it means you can cook food affordably, quickly and easily! I personally think the term "air fryer" is misleading because people get confused by the old-fashioned air fryer that your grandma might have in her pantry. The big difference, however, between these two types of fryer is that the modern air fryer does not require huge amounts of oil because it cooks food with only hot air—nothing else is required! So, hopefully you have learned that the Air Fryer cooks food by circulating hot air around using a convection mechanism. Enough of the interesting science, for now.

Did you forget to prepare something for dinner? No problem—the Air Fryer can cook such lovely delicious food in just moments! Such scrumptious food includes sizzling burgers and dry crispy fries– super affordable, quick & easy too! What's more? When your fryer finishes cooking, the latent heat inside keeps your food warm. I can confidently say that my air fryer has changed the way I cook because I now spend less time in the kitchen and more time doing the things I enjoy, like spending precious time with family and walking my dogs. In fact, even my weekly shop at my local grocery store is super cheap and easy. I fill my grocery basket to the brim with all kinds of locally sourced, affordable and easy to find ingredients which I whack into my Air Fryer, allowing me to whip up amazing meals for my family to enjoy.

Every week, I love frying a batch of burgers for a quick 'on-the-go' lunch after I take my grandchildren to school. What's great is the temperature control on my Air Fryer dial because it means I can have it all cooked for when I return home. In fact, I whack all manner of things in the frying basket on a low temperature because my Fryer keeps it warm for hours. This appliance has revolutionized how I cook, and I have even retired my once beloved Instant Pot back to the pantry.

BREAKFAST

Egg in a Hole

Preparation Time: 5 Minutes

Cooking Time: 5 Minutes

Servings: 1

Ingredients:

- One slice bread
- One teaspoon butter softened
- One egg
- One tablespoon shredded Cheddar cheese
- Two teaspoons diced ham

Directions:

1. Preheat the air fryer to 330°F (166°C). Place a baking dish in the air fryer basket.
2. On a flat surface, cut a hole in the bread slice's center with a 2½-inch-diameter biscuit cutter.
3. Spread the butter lightly on each side of the bread slice and transfer to the baking dish.
4. Crack the egg into the hole, then season as desired with salt and pepper. Scatter the shredded cheese and diced ham on top.
5. Bake in the preheated air fryer for 5 minutes until the bread is lightly browned and the egg is cooked to your preference.
6. Remove from the basket and serve hot.

Nutrition: Calories: 243 Fat: 14.5g Carbs: 15.4g Protein: 12.6g

Spinach and Bacon Roll-Ups

Preparation Time: 5 Minutes

Cooking Time: 8 to 9 Minutes

Servings: 4

Ingredients:

- Four flour tortillas (6- or 7-inch size)
- 4 slices Swiss cheese
- 1 cup baby spinach leaves
- Four slices of turkey bacon

Directions:

1. Preheat the air fryer to 390°F (199°C).
2. On a clean work surface, top each tortilla with one slice of cheese and ¼ cup of spinach, then tightly roll them up.
3. Wrap each tortilla with a strip of turkey bacon and secure with a toothpick.
4. Arrange the roll-ups in the air fryer basket, leaving space between each roll-up.
5. Air fry for 4 minutes. Flip the roll-ups with tongs and rearrange them for more even cooking. Air fry for another 4 to 5 minutes until the bacon is crisp.
6. Rest for 5 minutes and remove the toothpicks before serving.

Nutrition: Calories: 219 Fat: 11.6g Carbs: 16.3g Protein: 12.3g

Canadian Bacon Muffin Sandwiches

Preparation Time: 5 Minutes

Cooking Time: 8 Minutes

Servings: 4

Ingredients:

- 4 English muffins, split
- Eight slices of Canadian bacon
- Four slices cheese
- Cooking spray

Directions:

1. Preheat the air fryer to 370ºF (188ºC).
2. Make the sandwiches: Top each of 4 muffin halves with two slices of Canadian bacon, one piece of cheese, and finish with the remaining muffin half.
3. Put the sandwiches in the air fryer basket and spritz the tops with cooking spray.
4. Bake for 4 minutes. Flip the sandwiches and bake for additional 4 minutes.
5. Divide the sandwiches among four plates and serve warm.

Nutrition: Calories: 167 Fat: 8.3g Carbs: 12.8g Protein: 10.3g

Breakfast Cheese Sandwiches

Preparation Time: 5 Minutes

Cooking Time: 8 Minutes

Servings: 2

Ingredients:

- One teaspoon butter softened
- Four slices of bread
- Four slices smoked country ham
- 4 slices Cheddar cheese
- Four thick slices of tomato

Directions:

1. Preheat the air fryer to 370ºF (188ºC).
2. Spoon ½ teaspoon of butter onto one side of 2 slices of bread and spread it all over.
3. Assemble the sandwiches: Top each of 2 slices of unbuttered bread with two slices of tomato, two ham, and two slices of cheese. Place the remaining two slices of bread on top, butter-side up.
4. Arrange the sandwiches in the air fryer basket, buttered side down.
5. Bake for 8 minutes until the sandwiches are golden brown on both sides and the cheese has melted, flipping the sandwiches halfway through.

6. Allow cooling for 5 minutes beforehand slicing to serve.

Nutrition: Calories: 363 Fat: 29.1g Carbs: 17.3g Protein: 4.1g

Air Fryer Baked Eggs

Preparation Time: 5 Minutes

Cooking Time: 6 Minutes

Servings: 2

Ingredients:

- Two large eggs
- Two tablespoons half-and-half
- Two teaspoons shredded Cheddar cheese
- Salt and freshly ground black pepper
- Cooking spray

Directions:

1. Preheat the air fryer to 330ºF (166ºC).
2. Spritz two ramekins lightly with cooking spray. Crack an egg into each ramekin.
3. Top each egg with one tablespoon of half-and-half and one teaspoon of Cheddar cheese. Sprinkle with salt and black pepper. Stir the egg mixture with a fork until well combined.
4. Place the ramekins in the air fryer basket and bake for 6 minutes until set. Check for doneness and cook for 1 minute as needed.
5. Allow cooling for 5 minutes in the basket before removing and serving.

Nutrition: Calories: 243 Fat: 14.5g Carbs: 15.4g Protein: 12.6g

Peppered Maple Bacon Knots

Preparation Time: 5 Minutes

Cooking Time: 7 to 8 Minutes

Servings: 6

Ingredients:

- 1-pound (454 g) maple smoked center-cut bacon
- ¼ cup maple syrup
- ¼ cup brown sugar
- Coarsely cracked black peppercorns, to taste

Directions:

1. Preheat the air fryer to 390ºF (199ºC).
2. On a clean work surface, tie each bacon strip in a loose knot.
3. Mixing the maple syrup and brown sugar in a bowl. Generously brush this mixture over the bacon knots.
4. Working in batches, arrange the bacon knots in the air fryer basket. Sprinkle with the coarsely cracked black peppercorns.
5. Air fry for 5 minutes. Flip the bacon knots, continue cooking for 2 to 3 minutes more, or wait until the bacon is crisp.
6. Remove from the basket to a paper towel-lined plate. Repeat with the remaining bacon knots.

7. Let the bacon knots cool for a few minutes and serve warm.

Nutrition: Calories: 167 Fat: 8.3g Carbs: 12.8g Protein: 10.3g

Glazed Strawberry Toast

Preparation Time: 5 Minutes

Cooking Time: 8 Minutes

Servings: 4

Ingredients:

- Four slices bread, ½-inch thick
- 1 cup sliced strawberries
- One teaspoon sugar
- Cooking spray

Directions:

1. Preheat the air fryer to 375ºF (191ºC).
2. On a clean work surface, lay the bread slices and spritz one side of each piece of bread with cooking spray.
3. Put the bread slices in the air fryer basket, sprayed side down. Top with the strawberries and a sprinkle of sugar.
4. Air fry for 8 minutes until the toast is well browned on each side.
5. Remove from the air fryer basket to a plate and serve.

Nutrition: Calories: 67 Fat: 0.7gCarbs: 13.2g Protein: 2.0g

Cinnamon Sweet Potato Chips

Preparation Time: 5 Minutes

Cooking Time: 8 Minutes

Servings: 6 to 8

Ingredients:

- One small sweet potato, cut into 3/8-inch-thick slices
- Two tablespoons olive oil
- 1 to 2 teaspoon ground cinnamon

Directions:

1. Preheat the air fryer to 390ºF (199ºC).
2. Add the sweet potato slices and olive oil in a bowl and toss to coat. Fold in the cinnamon and stir to combine.
3. Arrange the sweet potato slices in a single layer in the air fryer basket.
4. Air fry for 8 minutes, or until the chips are crisp. Shake the basket halfway through.
5. Remove from the air fryer basket, then allow it to cool for 5 minutes before serving.

Nutrition: Calories: 101 Fat: 3.2g Carbs: 15.1g Protein: 4.1g

Ham and Cheese Toast

Preparation Time: 5 Minutes

Cooking Time: 6 Minutes

Servings: 1

Ingredients:

- One slice bread
- One teaspoon butter, at room temperature
- One egg
- Two teaspoons diced ham
- One tablespoon grated Cheddar cheese

Directions:

1. Preheat the air fryer to 325ºF (163ºC).
2. On a clean work surface, use a 2½-inch biscuit cutter to make a hole in the center of the bread slice with about ½-inch of bread remaining.
3. Spread the butter on both sides of the bread slice. Crack the egg into the hole, then season with salt and pepper to taste.
4. Transfer the bread to the air fryer basket. Air fry for 5 minutes. Scatter the cheese and diced ham on top and continue to cook for an additional 1 minute until the egg is set and the cheese has melted.
5. Remove the toast from the basket to a plate and let cool for 5 minutes before serving.

Nutrition: Calories: 540 Fat: 6.2g Carbs: 96.0g Protein: 29.6g

Eggs in Bell Pepper Rings

Preparation Time: 5 Minutes

Cooking Time: 10-16 Minutes

Servings: 4

Ingredients:

- One large bell pepper, cut into four ¾-inch rings
- Four eggs
- Salt and freshly ground black pepper
- Two teaspoons salsa
- Cooking spray

Directions:

1. Warm up the air fryer to 350ºF (177ºC). Coat a baking pan lightly with cooking spray.
2. Put two bell pepper rings in the prepared baking pan. Crack one egg into each bell pepper ring and sprinkle with salt and pepper. Top each egg with ½ teaspoon of salsa.
3. Put the baking pan in the air fryer basket and air fry for 5 to 8 minutes, or wait until the eggs are cooked to your desired doneness.
4. Remove from the pan to a plate and repeat with the remaining bell pepper rings, eggs, and salsa.
5. Serve warm.

Nutrition: Calories: 243 Fat: 14.5g Carbs: 15.4g Protein: 12.6g

LUNCH

Delicious Chicken Fajita

Preparation Time: 10 minutes

Cooking Time: 18 minutes

Servings: 4

Ingredients:

- 1 lb chicken breast, boneless, skinless & sliced
- 1/8 tsp cayenne
- 1 tsp cumin
- 2 tsp chili powder
- 2 tsp olive oil
- 1 onion, sliced
- 2 bell peppers, sliced
- Pepper
- Salt

Directions:

1. Add chicken, onion, and sliced bell peppers into the mixing bowl. Add cayenne, cumin, chili powder, oil, pepper, and salt and toss well.
2. Add chicken mixture into the air fryer basket and slide the basket into the air fryer.
3. Cook at 360 F for 15-20 minutes. Stir halfway through.
4. Serve and enjoy.

Nutrition: Calories 186 Fat 5.7 g Carbohydrates 8.1 g Sugar 4.3 g Protein 25.2 g Cholesterol 73 mg

Parmesan Chicken Wings

Preparation Time: 10 minutes

Cooking Time: 25 minutes

Servings 4

Ingredients:

- 1 1/2 lbs chicken wings
- 3/4 tbsp garlic powder
- 1/4 cup parmesan cheese, grated
- 2 tbsp arrowroot powder
- Pepper
- Salt

Directions:

1. Preheat the cosori air fryer to 380 F.
2. In a large bowl, mix together garlic powder, parmesan cheese, arrowroot powder, pepper, and salt. Add chicken wings and toss until well coated.
3. Add chicken wings into the air fryer basket. Spray top of chicken wings with cooking spray.
4. Select chicken and press start. Shake air fryer basket halfway through.
5. Serve and enjoy.

Nutrition: Calories 386 Fat 15.3 g Carbohydrates 5.6 g Sugar 0.4 g Protein 53.5 g Cholesterol 160 mg

Western Chicken Wings

Preparation Time: 10 minutes

Cooking Time: 15 minutes

Servings: 4

Ingredients:

- 2 lbs chicken wings
- 1 tsp Herb de Provence
- 1 tsp paprika
- 1/2 cup parmesan cheese, grated
- Pepper
- Salt

Directions:

1. Add cheese, paprika, herb de Provence, pepper, and salt into the large mixing bowl. Add chicken wings into the bowl and toss well to coat.
2. Preheat the cosori air fryer to 350 F.
3. Add chicken wings into the air fryer basket. Spray top of chicken wings with cooking spray.
4. Cook chicken wings for 15 minutes. Turn chicken wings halfway through.
5. Serve and enjoy.

Nutrition: Calories 473 Fat 19.6 g Carbohydrates 0.8 g Sugar 0.1 g Protein 69.7 g Cholesterol 211 mg

Perfect Whole Chicken

Preparation Time: 10 minutes

Cooking Time: 50 minutes

Servings: 4

Ingredients:

- 3 lbs whole chicken, remove giblets & pat dry with a paper towel
- 1 tsp Italian seasoning
- 1/2 tsp dried rosemary
- 1/2 tsp dry thyme
- 1/2 tsp garlic powder
- 1/2 tsp onion powder
- 1/4 tsp paprika
- 1 tbsp olive oil
- Pepper
- Salt

Directions:

1. In a small bowl, mix together oil, Italian seasoning, rosemary, thyme, garlic powder, onion powder, paprika, pepper, and salt.
2. Rub oil and spice mixture all over the chicken.
3. Place chicken breast side down in the air fryer basket.
4. Roast chicken at 360 F for 30 minutes.

---

5. After 30 minutes flip chicken and roast for 20 minutes more.
6. Allow cooling chicken for 10 minutes.
7. Slice and serve.

Nutrition: Calories 683 Fat 29.1 g Carbohydrates 0.9 g Sugar 0.3 g Protein 98.6 g Cholesterol 304 mg

Juicy Chicken Breasts

Preparation Time: 10 minutes

Cooking Time: 10 minutes

Servings 4

Ingredients:

- 4 chicken breasts, boneless
- 1/8 tsp cayenne pepper
- 1/2 tsp paprika
- 1/2 tsp dried parsley
- 1/2 tsp onion powder

- 1/2 tsp garlic powder
- Pepper
- Salt

Directions:

1. Add 6 cups warm water and 1/4 cup kosher salt into the large bowl and stir until salt dissolve.
2. Add chicken breasts into the water and place a bowl in the refrigerator for 2 hours to brine.
3. After 2 hours remove water and pat dry chicken breasts with paper towels.
4. In a small bowl, mix together garlic powder, onion powder, dried parsley, paprika, cayenne pepper, and pepper.
5. Spray chicken breasts with cooking spray then rub with spice mixture.
6. Preheat the cosori air fryer to 380 F.
7. Place chicken breasts into the air fryer basket and cook for 10 minutes. Turn chicken breasts halfway through.
8. Serve and enjoy.

Nutrition: Calories 281 Fat 10.9 g Carbohydrates 0.7 g Sugar 0.2 g Protein 42.4 g Cholesterol 130 mg

Flavors Dijon Chicken

Preparation Time: 10 minutes

Cooking Time: 14 minutes

Servings 6

Ingredients:

- 1 1/2 lbs chicken breasts, boneless
- 1/4 tsp cayenne
- 1 tsp Italian seasoning
- 1 tbsp coconut aminos
- 1 tbsp fresh lemon juice
- 1 tbsp Dijon mustard
- 1/2 cup mayonnaise
- 1/2 tsp pepper
- 1 tsp sea salt

Directions:

1. In a small bowl, mix together mayonnaise, cayenne, Italian seasoning, coconut amino, lemon juice, mustard, pepper, and salt.
2. Add chicken into the zip-lock bag. Pour mayonnaise mixture over chicken and mix well.
3. Seal ziplock bag and place in the refrigerator overnight.
4. Preheat the cosori air fryer to 400 F.

5. Place marinated chicken in the air fryer basket and cook for 14 minutes. Turn chicken halfway through.
6. Serve and enjoy.

Nutrition: Calories 300 Fat 15.3 g Carbohydrates 5.6 g Sugar 1.4 g Protein 33.2 g Cholesterol 107 mg

Crispy Crusted Chicken Tenders

Preparation Time: 10 minutes

Cooking Time: 10 minutes

Servings: 6

Ingredients:

- 2 eggs, lightly beaten
- 6 chicken tenders
- 1/2 tsp onion powder
- 1/2 tsp garlic powder
- 1 tsp paprika
- 1 cup pork rinds, crushed
- 1 tsp salt

Directions:

1. In a shallow bowl, mix together crushed pork rinds, paprika, garlic powder, onion powder, and salt.
2. In a separate shallow bowl, add beaten eggs.
3. Dip chicken tenders in eggs then coat with crushed pork rind mixture.
4. Place coated chicken tenders in the air fryer basket and cook at 400 F for 10 minutes. Turn chicken tenders halfway through.
5. Serve and enjoy.

Nutrition: Calories 66 Fat 3.5 g Carbohydrates 0.6 g Sugar 0.3 g Protein 7.9 g Cholesterol 72 mg

Tender & Juicy Cornish Hens

Preparation Time: 10 minutes

Cooking Time: 45 minutes

Servings: 4

Ingredients:

- 2 Cornish game hens
- 1/2 tsp dried thyme
- 1/2 tsp dried oregano
- 1/2 tsp dried basil
- 1 tsp paprika
- 1 tsp garlic powder
- 1 tsp pepper
- 2 tbsp olive oil
- 1 tbsp kosher salt

Directions:

1. In a small bowl, mix together oil, garlic powder, paprika, basil, oregano, thyme, pepper, and salt.
2. Rub oil spice mixture all over hens.
3. Place hens in the air fryer basket breast side down and cook for 35 minutes at 360 F.
4. Turn the hens and cook for 10 minutes more.
5. Serve and enjoy.

Nutrition: Calories 400 Fat 30.5 g Carbohydrates 1.4 g Sugar 0.2 g Protein 28.9 g Cholesterol 168 mg

Flavors & Crisp Chicken Thighs

Preparation Time: 10 minutes

Cooking Time: 22 minutes

Servings: 4

Ingredients:

- 4 chicken thighs, bone-in, skin-on, & remove excess fat
- 3/4 tsp onion powder
- 1/2 tsp oregano
- 3/4 tsp garlic powder
- 1 tsp paprika
- 1 tbsp olive oil
- 1/2 tsp kosher salt

Directions:

1. Preheat the cosori air fryer to 380 F.
2. Add chicken thighs into the large zip-lock bag. Add spices and oil over chicken.
3. Seal zip-lock bag and shake well to coat.
4. Place chicken thighs in the air fryer basket skin side down and cook for 12 minutes.
5. Turn chicken thighs and cook for 10 minutes more.
6. Serve and enjoy.

Nutrition: Calories 313 Fat 14.3 g Carbohydrates 1.2 g Sugar 0.4 g Protein 42.5 g Cholesterol 130 mg

Cheesy Cauliflower Pizza Crust

Preparation time: 15 minutes

Cooking time: 11 minutes

Servings: 2

Ingredients:

- 1 (12-ounce) steamer bag cauliflower
- ½ cup shredded sharp Cheddar cheese
- 1 large egg
- 2 tablespoons blanched finely ground almond flour
- 1 teaspoon Italian blend seasoning

Directions:

1. Cook cauliflower according to package instructions. Remove from bag and place into cheesecloth or paper towel to remove excess water. Place cauliflower into a large bowl.
2. Add cheese, egg, almond flour, and Italian seasoning to the bowl and mix well.
3. Cut a piece of parchment to fit your air fryer basket. Press cauliflower into 6" round circle. Place into the air fryer basket.
4. Adjust the temperature to 360°F and set the timer for 11 minutes.
5. After 7 minutes, flip the pizza crust.
6. Add preferred toppings to pizza. Place back into air fryer basket and cook an additional 4 minutes

or until fully cooked and golden. Serve immediately.

Nutrition: Calories: 230 Protein: 14.9 g Fiber: 4.7 g Net carbohydrates: 5.3 g Fat: 14.2 g Sodium: 257 mg Carbohydrates: 10.0 g Sugar: 4.2 g

DINNER

Perfect Chicken Thighs Dinner

Preparation Time: 10 minutes

Cooking Time: 15 minutes

Servings: 4

Ingredients:

- 4 chicken thighs, bone-in & skinless
- 1/4 tsp ground ginger
- 2 tsp paprika
- 2 tsp garlic powder
- 1/4 tsp pepper
- 1 tsp salt

Directions:

1. Preheat the cosori air fryer to 400 F.
2. In a small bowl, mix together ginger, paprika, garlic powder, pepper, and salt and rub all over chicken thighs.
3. Spray chicken thighs with cooking spray.
4. Place chicken thighs into the air fryer basket and cook for 10 minutes.
5. Turn chicken thighs and cook for 5 minutes more.
6. Serve and enjoy.

Nutrition: Calories 286 Fat 11 g Carbohydrates 1.8 g Sugar 0.5 g Protein 42.7 g Cholesterol 130 mg

Quiche-Stuffed Peppers

Preparation time: 5 minutes

Cooking time: 15 minutes

Servings: 2

Ingredients:

- 2 medium green bell peppers
- 3 large eggs
- ¼ cup full-fat ricotta cheese
- ¼ cup diced yellow onion
- ½ cup chopped broccoli
- ½ cup shredded medium Cheddar cheese

Directions:

1. Cut the tops off of the peppers and remove the seeds and white membranes with a small knife.
2. In a medium bowl, whisk eggs and ricotta.
3. Add onion and broccoli. Pour the egg and vegetable mixture evenly into each pepper. Top with Cheddar. Place peppers into a 4-cup round baking dish and place into the air fryer basket.
4. Adjust the temperature to 350°F and set the timer for 15 minutes.
5. Eggs will be mostly firm and peppers tender when fully cooked. Serve immediately.

Nutrition: Calories: 314 Protein: 21.6 g Fiber: 3.0 g Net carbohydrates: 7.8 g Fat: 18.7 g Sodium: 325 mg

Carbohydrates: 10.8 g Sugar: 4.5 g

Roasted Garlic White Zucchini Rolls

Preparation time: 20 minutes

Cooking time: 20 minutes

Servings: 4

Ingredients:

- 2 medium zucchini
- 2 tablespoons unsalted butter
- ¼ white onion, peeled and diced
- ½ teaspoon finely minced roasted garlic
- ¼ cup heavy cream
- 2 tablespoons vegetable broth
- ⅛ teaspoon xanthan gum
- ½ cup full-fat ricotta cheese
- ¼ teaspoon salt
- ½ teaspoon garlic powder
- ¼ teaspoon dried oregano
- 2 cups spinach, chopped
- ½ cup sliced baby portobello mushrooms
- ¾ cup shredded mozzarella cheese, divided

Directions:

1. Using a mandoline or sharp knife, slice zucchini into long strips lengthwise. Place strips between paper towels to absorb moisture. Set aside.

2. In a medium saucepan over medium heat, melt butter. Add onion and sauté until fragrant. Add garlic and sauté 30 seconds.
3. Pour in heavy cream, broth, and xanthan gum. Turn off heat and whisk mixture until it begins to thicken, about 3 minutes.
4. In a medium bowl, add ricotta, salt, garlic powder, and oregano and mix well. Fold in spinach, mushrooms, and ½ cup mozzarella.
5. Pour half of the sauce into a 6" round baking pan. To assemble the rolls, place two strips of zucchini on a work surface. Spoon 2 tablespoons of ricotta mixture onto the slices and roll up. Place seam side down on top of sauce. Repeat with remaining ingredients.
6. Pour remaining sauce over the rolls and sprinkle with remaining mozzarella. Cover with foil and place into the air fryer basket.
7. Adjust the temperature to 350°F and set the timer for 20 minutes.
8. In the last 5 minutes, remove the foil to brown the cheese. Serve immediately.

Nutrition: Calories: 245 Protein: 10.5 g Fiber: 1.8 g Net carbohydrates: 5.3 g Fat: 18.9 g Sodium: 346 mg Carbohydrates: 7.1 g Sugar: 3.8 g

Spicy Parmesan Artichokes

Preparation time: 10 minutes

Cooking time: 10 minutes

Servings: 4

Ingredients:

- 2 medium artichokes, trimmed and quartered, center removed
- 2 tablespoons coconut oil
- 1 large egg, beaten
- ½ cup grated vegetarian Parmesan cheese
- ¼ cup blanched finely ground almond flour
- ½ teaspoon crushed red pepper flakes

Directions:

1. In a large bowl, toss artichokes in coconut oil and then dip each piece into the egg.
2. Mix the Parmesan and almond flour in a large bowl. Add artichoke pieces and toss to cover as completely as possible, sprinkle with pepper flakes. Place into the air fryer basket.
3. Adjust the temperature to 400°F and set the timer for 10 minutes.
4. Toss the basket two times during cooking. Serve warm.

Nutrition: Calories: 189 Protein: 7.9 g Fiber: 4.2 g Net carbohydrates: 5.8 g Fat: 13.5 g Sodium: 294 mg Carbohydrates: 10.0 g Sugar: 0.9 g

Zucchini Cauliflower Fritters

Preparation time: 15 minutes

Cooking time: 12 minutes

Servings: 2

Ingredients:

- 1 (12-ounce) cauliflower steamer bag
- 1 medium zucchini, shredded
- ¼ cup almond flour
- 1 large egg
- ½ teaspoon garlic powder
- ¼ cup grated vegetarian Parmesan cheese

Directions:

1. Cook cauliflower according to package instructions and drain excess moisture in cheesecloth or paper towel. Place into a large bowl.
2. Place zucchini into paper towel and pat down to remove excess moisture. Add to bowl with cauliflower. Add remaining ingredients.
3. Divide the mixture evenly and form four patties. Press into ¼"-thick patties. Place each into the air fryer basket.
4. Adjust the temperature to 320°F and set the timer for 12 minutes.

5. Fritters will be firm when fully cooked. Allow to cool 5 minutes before moving. Serve warm.

Nutrition: Calories: 217 Protein: 13.7 g Fiber: 6.5 g Net carbohydrates: 8.5 g Fat: 12.0 g Sodium: 263 mg Carbohydrates: 16.1 g Sugar: 6.8 g

Basic Spaghetti Squash

Preparation time: 10 minutes

Cooking time: 45 minutes

Servings: 2

Ingredients:

- ½ large spaghetti squash
- 1 tablespoon coconut oil
- 2 tablespoons salted butter, melted
- ½ teaspoon garlic powder
- 1 teaspoon dried parsley

Directions:

1. Brush shell of spaghetti squash with coconut oil. Place the skin side down and brush the inside with butter. Sprinkle with garlic powder and parsley.
2. Place squash with the skin side down into the air fryer basket.
3. Adjust the temperature to 350°F and set the timer for 30 minutes.
4. When the timer beeps, flip the squash so skin side is up and cook an additional 15 minutes or until fork tender. Serve warm.

Nutrition: Calories: 182 Protein: 1.9 g Fiber: 3.9 g Net carbohydrates: 14.3 g Fat: 11.7 g Sodium: 134 mg Carbohydrates: 18.2 g Sugar: 7.0 g

Spaghetti Squash Alfredo

Preparation time: 10 minutes

Cooking time: 15 minutes

Servings: 2

Ingredients:

- ½ large cooked spaghetti squash
- 2 tablespoons salted butter, melted
- ½ cup low-carb Alfredo sauce
- ¼ cup grated vegetarian Parmesan cheese
- ½ teaspoon garlic powder
- 1 teaspoon dried parsley
- ¼ teaspoon ground peppercorn
- ½ cup shredded Italian blend cheese

Directions:

1. Using a fork, remove the strands of spaghetti squash from the shell. Place into a large bowl with butter and Alfredo sauce. Sprinkle with Parmesan, garlic powder, parsley, and peppercorn.

2. Pour into a 4-cup round baking dish and top with shredded cheese. Place dish into the air fryer basket.

3. Adjust the temperature to 320°F and set the timer for 15 minutes.

4. When finished, cheese will be golden and bubbling. Serve immediately.

Nutrition: Calories: 375 Protein: 13.5 g Fiber: 4.0 g Net carbohydrates: 20.1 g Fat: 24.2 g Sodium: 950 mg Carbohydrates: 24.1 g Sugar: 8.0 g

Caprese Eggplant Stacks

Preparation time: 5 minutes

Cooking time: 12 minutes

Servings: 4

Ingredients:

- 1 medium eggplant, cut into ¼" slices
- 2 large tomatoes, cut into ¼" slices
- 4 ounces fresh mozzarella, cut into ½-ounce slices
- 2 tablespoons olive oil
- ¼ cup fresh basil, sliced

Directions:

1. In a 6" round baking dish, place four slices of eggplant on the bottom. Place a slice of tomato on top of each eggplant round, then mozzarella, then eggplant. Repeat as necessary.
2. Drizzle with olive oil. Cover dish with foil and place dish into the air fryer basket.
3. Adjust the temperature to 350°F and set the timer for 12 minutes.
4. When done, eggplant will be tender. Garnish with fresh basil to serve.

Nutrition: Calories: 195 Protein: 8.5 g Fiber: 5.2 g Net carbohydrates: 7.5 g Fat: 12.7 g Sodium: 184 mg Carbohydrates: 12.7 g Sugar: 7.5 g

Crustless Spinach Cheese Pie

Preparation time: 10 minutes

Cooking time: 20 minutes

Servings: 4

Ingredients:

- 6 large eggs
- ¼ cup heavy whipping cream
- 1 cup frozen chopped spinach, drained
- 1 cup shredded sharp Cheddar cheese
- ¼ cup diced yellow onion

Directions:

1. In a medium bowl, whisk eggs and add cream. Add remaining ingredients to bowl.
2. Pour into a 6" round baking dish. Place into the air fryer basket.
3. Adjust the temperature to 320°F and set the timer for 20 minutes.
4. Eggs will be firm and slightly browned when cooked. Serve immediately.

Nutrition: Calories: 288 Protein: 18.0 g Fiber: 1.3 g Net carbohydrates: 2.6 g Fat: 20.0 g Sodium: 322 mg Carbohydrates: 3.9 g Sugar: 1.5 g

Broccoli Crust Pizza

Preparation time: 15 minutes

Cooking time: 13 minutes

Servings: 4

Ingredients:

- 3 cups riced broccoli, steamed and drained well
- 1 large egg
- ½ cup grated vegetarian Parmesan cheese
- 3 tablespoons low-carb Alfredo sauce
- ½ cup shredded mozzarella cheese

Directions:

1. In a large bowl, mix broccoli, egg, and Parmesan.
2. Cut a piece of parchment to fit your air fryer basket. Press out the pizza mixture to fit on the parchment, working in two batches if necessary. Place into the air fryer basket.
3. Adjust the temperature to 370°F and set the timer for 5 minutes.
4. When the timer beeps, the crust should be firm enough to flip. If not, add 2 additional minutes. Flip crust.
5. Top with Alfredo sauce and mozzarella. Return to the air fryer basket and cook an additional 7 minutes or until cheese is golden and bubbling. Serve warm.

Nutrition: Calories: 136 Protein: 9.9 g Fiber: 2.3 g Net carbohydrates: 3.4 g Fat: 7.6 g Sodium: 421 mg

Carbohydrates: 5.7 g Sugar: 1.1 g

SIDES

Squash and Cumin Chili

Preparation Time: 10 Minutes

Cooking Time: 16 Minutes

Servings: 4

Ingredients:

- One medium butternut squash
- One teaspoon cumin seed
- One large pinch of chili flakes
- One tablespoon olive oil
- One and ½ ounces pine nuts
- One small bunch of fresh coriander, chopped

Directions:

1. Take the squash and slice it
2. Remove seeds and cut into smaller chunks
3. Take a bowl and add chunked squash, spice, and oil
4. Mix well
5. Pre-heat your Fryer to 360 degrees F and add the squash to the cooking basket
6. Roast for 20 minutes. Ensure to shake the basket from time to time to avoid burning
7. Take a pan and place it over medium heat, add pine nuts to the pan, and dry toast for 2 minutes
8. Sprinkle nuts on top of the squash and serve
9. Enjoy!

Nutrition: Calories: 414 Fat: 15g Carbohydrates: 10g Protein: 16g

Fried Up Avocados

Preparation Time: 10 Minutes

Cooking Time: 20 Minutes

Servings: 6

Ingredients:

- ½ cup almond meal
- ½ teaspoon salt
- 1 Hass avocado, peeled, pitted, and sliced
- Aquafaba from one bean can (bean liquid)

Directions:

1. Take a shallow bowl and add almond meal, salt
2. Pour aquafaba in another bowl, dredge avocado slices in aquafaba and then into the crumbs to get a nice coating
3. Assemble them in a single layer in your Air Fryer cooking basket, don't overlap
4. Cook for 10 minutes at 390 degrees F, give the basket a shake, and cook for 5 minutes more
5. Serve and enjoy!

Nutrition: Calories: 356 Fat: 14g Carbohydrates: 8g Protein: 23g

Hearty Green Beans

Preparation Time: 5 Minutes

Cooking Time: 10 to 15 Minutes

Servings: 6

Ingredients:

- 1-pound green beans washed and de-stemmed
- One lemon
- Pinch of salt
- ¼ teaspoon oil

Directions:

1. Add beans to your Air Fryer cooking basket
2. Squeeze a few drops of lemon
3. Season with salt and pepper
4. Drizzle olive oil on top
5. Cook for 10-12 minutes at 400 degrees F
6. Once done, serve and enjoy!

Nutrition: Calories: 84 Fat: 5g Carbohydrates: 7g Protein: 2g

Parmesan Cabbage Wedges

Preparation Time: 5 Minutes

Cooking Time: 20 Minutes

Servings: 4

Ingredients:

- ½ a head cabbage
- 2 cups parmesan
- Four tablespoons melted butter
- Salt and pepper to taste

Directions:

1. Preheat your Air Fryer to 380-degree F.
2. Take a container and add melted butter, and season with salt and pepper.
3. Cover cabbages with your melted butter.
4. Coat cabbages with parmesan.
5. Transfer the coated cabbages to your Air Fryer and bake for 20 minutes.
6. Serve with cheesy sauce and enjoy!

Nutrition: Calories: 108 Fat: 7g Carbohydrates: 11g Protein: 2g

Extreme Zucchini Fries

Preparation Time: 10 Minutes

Cooking Time: 15 to 20 Minutes

Servings: 4

Ingredients:

- Three medium zucchinis, sliced
- Two egg whites
- ½ cup seasoned almond meal
- Two tablespoons grated parmesan cheese
- ¼ teaspoon garlic powder

Directions:

1. Pre-heat your Fryer to 425-degree F.
2. Take the Air Fryer cooking basket and place a cooling rack.
3. Coat the rack with cooking spray.
4. Take a bowl, add egg whites, beat it well, and season with some pepper and salt.
5. Take another bowl and add garlic powder, cheese, and almond meal
6. Take the Zucchini sticks and dredge them in the egg and finally breadcrumbs.
7. Transfer the Zucchini to your cooking basket and spray a bit of oil.
8. Bake for 20 minutes and serve with Ranch sauce.
9. Enjoy!

Nutrition: Calories: 367 Fat: 28g Carbohydrates: 5g
Protein: 4g

Easy Fried Tomatoes

Preparation Time: 5 Minutes

Cooking Time: 10 Minutes

Servings: 3

Ingredients:

- One green tomato
- ¼ tablespoon Creole seasoning
- Salt and pepper to taste
- ¼ cup almond flour
- ½ cup buttermilk

Directions:

1. Add flour to your plate and take another plate and add buttermilk
2. Cut tomatoes and season with salt and pepper
3. Make a mix of creole seasoning and crumbs
4. Take tomato slice and cover with flour, place in buttermilk and then into crumbs
5. Repeat with all tomatoes
6. Preheat your fryer to 400-degree F
7. Cook the tomato slices for 5 minutes
8. Serve with basil and enjoy!

Nutrition: Calories: 166 Fat: 12g Carbohydrates: 11g Protein: 3g

Roasted Up Brussels

Preparation Time: 10 Minutes

Cooking Time: 15 Minutes

Servings: 4

Ingredients:

- One block Brussels sprouts
- ½ teaspoon garlic
- Two teaspoons olive oil
- ½ teaspoon pepper
- Salt as needed

Directions:

1. Pre-heat your Fryer to 390-degree F.
2. Remove leaves off the chokes, leaving only the head.
3. Wash and dry the sprouts well.
4. Make a mixture of olive oil, salt, and pepper with garlic.
5. Cover sprouts with the marinade and let them rest for 5 minutes.
6. Transfer coated sprouts to Air Fryer and cook for 15 minutes.
7. Serve and enjoy!

Nutrition: Calories: 43 Fat: 2g Carbohydrates: 5g Protein: 2g

Roasted Brussels and Pine Nuts

Preparation Time: 10 Minutes

Cooking Time: 35 Minutes

Servings: 6

Ingredients:

- 15 ounces Brussels sprouts
- One tablespoon olive oil
- One and ¾ ounces raisins, drained
- Juice of 1 orange
- One and ¾ ounces toasted pine nuts

Directions:

1. Take a pot of boiling water, then add sprouts and boil them for 4 minutes.
2. Transfer the sprouts to cold water and drain them well.
3. Place them in a freezer and cool them.
4. Take your raisins and soak them in orange juice for 20 minutes.
5. Warm your Air Fryer to a temperature of 392-degree F.
6. Take a pan and pour oil, and stir the sprouts.
7. Take the sprouts and transfer them to your Air Fryer.
8. Roast for 15 minutes.

9. Serve the sprouts with pine nuts, orange juice, and raisins!

Nutrition: Calories: 260 Fat: 20g Carbohydrates: 10g Protein: 7g

Low-Calorie Beets Dish

Preparation Time: 10 Minutes

Cooking Time: 10 Minutes

Servings: 2

Ingredients:

- Four whole beets
- One tablespoon balsamic vinegar
- One tablespoon olive oil
- Salt and pepper to taste
- Two springs rosemary

Directions:

1. Wash your beets and peel them
2. Cut beets into cubes
3. Take a bowl and mix in rosemary, pepper, salt, vinegar
4. Cover beets with the prepared sauce
5. Coat the beets with olive oil
6. Pre-heat your Fryer to 400-degree F
7. Transfer beets to Air Fryer cooking basket and cook for 10 minutes
8. Serve with your cheese sauce and enjoy!

Nutrition: Calories: 149 Fat: 1g Carbohydrates: 5g Protein: 30g

Broccoli and Parmesan Dish

Preparation Time: 5 Minutes

Cooking Time: 20 Minutes

Servings: 4

Ingredients:

- One fresh head broccoli
- One tablespoon olive oil
- One lemon, juiced
- Salt and pepper to taste
- 1-ounce parmesan cheese, grated

Directions:

1. Wash broccoli thoroughly and cut them into florets.
2. Add the listed ingredients to your broccoli and mix well.
3. Preheat your fryer to 365-degree F.
4. Air fry broccoli for 20 minutes.
5. Serve and enjoy!

Nutrition: Calories: 114 Fat: 6g Carbohydrates: 10 g Protein: 7g

DESSERTS

Buttery Chocolate Cake

Preparation time: 20 minutes

Cooking time: 11 minutes

Servings: 4

Ingredients:

- 2½ ounces (71 g) butter, at room temperature
- 3 ounces (85 g) chocolate, unsweetened
- 2 eggs, beaten
- ½ cup Swerve
- ½ cup almond flour
- 1 teaspoon rum extract
- 1 teaspoon vanilla extract

Directions:

1. Begin by preheating your Air Fryer to 370 degrees F (188ºC). Spritz the sides and bottom of four ramekins with cooking spray.
2. Melt the butter and chocolate in a microwave-safe bowl. Mix the eggs and Swerve until frothy.
3. Pour the butter/chocolate mixture into the egg mixture. Stir in the almond flour, rum extract, and vanilla extract. Mix until everything is well incorporated.

4. Scrape the batter into the prepared ramekins. Bake in the preheated Air Fryer for 9 to 11 minutes.
5. Let stand for 2 to 3 minutes. Invert on a plate while warm and serve. Bon appétit!

Nutrition: calories: 364 fat: 33g protein: 8g carbs: 9g net carbs: 4g fiber: 5g

Chocolate Butter Cake

Preparation time: 30 minutes

Cooking time: 22 minutes

Servings: 10

Ingredients:

- 1 cup no-sugar-added peanut butter
- 1¼ cups monk fruit
- 3 eggs
- 1 cup almond flour
- 1 teaspoon baking powder
- ¼ teaspoon kosher salt
- 1 cup unsweetened bakers' chocolate, broken into chunks

Directions:

1. Start by preheating your Air Fryer to 350 degrees F (180ºC). Now, spritz the sides and bottom of a baking pan with cooking spray.
2. In a mixing dish, thoroughly combine the peanut butter with the monk fruit until creamy. Next, fold in the egg and beat until fluffy.
3. After that, stir in the almond flour, baking powder, salt, and bakers'chocolate. Mix until everything is well combined.
4. Bake in the preheated Air Fryer for 20 to 22 minutes. Transfer to a wire rack to cool before slicing and serving. Bon appétit!

Nutrition: Calories: 207 Fat: 17g Protein: 8g Carbs: 6g Net carbs: 3gFiber: 3g

Butter Chocolate Cake with Pecan

Preparation time: 30 minutes

Cooking time: 22 minutes

Servings: 6

Ingredients:

- ½ cup butter, melted
- ½ cup Swerve
- 1 teaspoon vanilla essence
- 1 egg
- ½ cup almond flour
- ½ teaspoon baking powder
- ¼ cup cocoa powder
- ½ teaspoon ground cinnamon
- ¼ teaspoon fine sea salt
- 1 ounce (28 g) bakers' chocolate, unsweetened
- ¼ cup pecans, finely chopped

Directions:

1. Start by preheating your Air Fryer to 350 degrees F (180ºC). Now, lightly grease six silicone molds.

2. In a mixing dish, beat the melted butter with the Swerve until fluffy. Next, stir in the vanilla and egg and beat again.

3. After that, add the almond flour, baking powder, cocoa powder, cinnamon, and salt. Mix until everything is well combined.

4. Fold in the chocolate and pecans; mix to combine. Bake in the preheated Air Fryer for 20 to 22 minutes. Enjoy!

Nutrition: Calories: 253 At: 25g Protein: 4g Carbs: 6g Net carbs: 3g Fiber: 3g

Baked Cheesecake

Preparation time: 40 minutes

Cooking time: 35 minutes

Servings: 6

Ingredients:

- ½ cup almond flour
- 1½ tablespoons unsalted butter, melted
- 2 tablespoons erythritol
- 1 (8-ounce / 227-g) package cream cheese, softened
- ¼ cup powdered erythritol
- ½ teaspoon vanilla paste
- 1 egg, at room temperature
- Topping:
- 1½ cups sour cream
- 3 tablespoons powdered erythritol
- 1 teaspoon vanilla extract

Directions:

1. Thoroughly combine the almond flour, butter, and 2 tablespoons of erythritol in a mixing bowl. Press the mixture into the bottom of lightly greased custard cups.
2. Then, mix the cream cheese, ¼ cup of powdered erythritol, vanilla, and egg using an electric mixer on low speed. Pour the batter into the pan, covering the crust.

3. Bake in the preheated Air Fryer at 330 degrees F (166ºC) for 35 minutes until edges are puffed and the surface is firm.
4. Mix the sour cream, 3 tablespoons of powdered erythritol, and vanilla for the topping; spread over the crust and allow it to cool to room temperature.
5. Transfer to your refrigerator for 6 to 8 hours. Serve well chilled.

Nutrition: Calories: 306 Fat: 27g Protein: 8gCarbs: 9g Net carbs: 7g Fiber: 2g

Crusted Mini Cheesecake

Preparation time: 30 minutes

Cooking time: 18 minutes

Servings: 8

Ingredients:

- For the Crust:
- $1/_3$ teaspoon grated nutmeg
- 1½ tablespoons erythritol
- 1½ cups almond meal
- 8 tablespoons melted butter
- 1 teaspoon ground cinnamon
- A pinch of kosher salt, to taste
- For the Cheesecake:
- 2 eggs
- ½ cups unsweetened chocolate chips
- 1½ tablespoons sour cream
- 4 ounces (113 g) soft cheese
- ½ cup Swerve
- ½ teaspoon vanilla essence

Directions:

1. Firstly, line eight cups of mini muffin pan with paper liners.
2. To make the crust, mix the almond meal together with erythritol, cinnamon, nutmeg, and kosher salt.

3. Now, add melted butter and stir well to moisten the crumb mixture.
4. Divide the crust mixture among the muffin cups and press gently to make even layers.
5. In another bowl, whip together the soft cheese, sour cream and Swerve until uniform and smooth. Fold in the eggs and the vanilla essence.
6. Then, divide chocolate chips among the prepared muffin cups. Then, add the cheese mix to each muffin cup.
7. Bake for about 18 minutes at 345 degrees F (174ºC). Bake in batches if needed. To finish, transfer the mini cheesecakes to a cooling rack; store in the fridge.

Nutrition: Calories: 314 Fat: 29g Protein: 7g Carbs: 7g Net carbs: 4g Fiber: 3g

Creamy Cheese Cake

Preparation time: 1 hour

Cooking time: 37 minutes

Servings: 8

Ingredients:

- 1½ cups almond flour
- 3 ounces (85 g) Swerve
- ½ stick butter, melted
- 20 ounces (567 g) full-fat cream cheese
- ½ cup heavy cream
- 1¼ cups granulated Swerve
- 3 eggs, at room temperature
- 1 tablespoon vanilla essence
- 1 teaspoon grated lemon zest

Directions:

1. Coat the sides and bottom of a baking pan with a little flour.
2. In a mixing bowl, combine the almond flour and Swerve. Add the melted butter and mix until your mixture looks like bread crumbs.
3. Press the mixture into the bottom of the prepared pan to form an even layer. Bake at 330 degrees F (166ºC) for 7 minutes until golden brown. Allow it to cool completely on a wire rack.
4. Meanwhile, in a mixer fitted with the paddle attachment, prepare the filling by mixing the soft

cheese, heavy cream, and granulated Swerve; beat until creamy and fluffy.

5. Crack the eggs into the mixing bowl, one at a time; add the vanilla and lemon zest and continue to mix until fully combined.
6. Pour the prepared topping over the cooled crust and spread evenly.
7. Bake in the preheated Air Fryer at 330 degrees F (166ºC) for 25 to 30 minutes; leave it in the Air Fryer to keep warm for another 30 minutes.
8. Cover your cheesecake with plastic wrap. Place in your refrigerator and allow it to cool at least 6 hours or overnight. Serve well chilled.

Nutrition: Calories: 245 Fat: 21g Protein: 8g Carbs: 7g Net carbs: 5g Fiber: 2g

Air Fried Chocolate Brownies

Preparation time: 40 minutes
Cooking time: 35 minutes
Servings: 8
Ingredients:
- 5 ounces (142 g) unsweetened chocolate, chopped into chunks
- 2 tablespoons instant espresso powder
- 1 tablespoon cocoa powder, unsweetened

- ½ cup almond butter
- ½ cup almond meal
- ¾ cup Swerve
- 1 teaspoon pure coffee extract
- ½ teaspoon lime peel zest
- ¼ cup coconut flour
- 2 eggs plus 1 egg yolk
- ½ teaspoon baking soda
- ½ teaspoon baking powder
- ½ teaspoon ground cinnamon
- $1/_3$ teaspoon ancho chile powder
- For the Chocolate Mascarpone Frosting:
- 4 ounces (113 g) mascarpone cheese, at room temperature
- 1½ ounces (43 g) unsweetened chocolate chips
- 1½ cups Swerve
- ¼ cup unsalted butter, at room temperature
- 1 teaspoon vanilla paste
- A pinch of fine sea salt

Directions:

1. First of all, microwave the chocolate and almond butter until completely melted; allow the mixture to cool at room temperature.
2. Then, whisk the eggs, Swerve, cinnamon, espresso powder, coffee extract, ancho chile powder, and lime zest.

3. Next step, add the vanilla/egg mixture to the chocolate/butter mixture. Stir in the almond meal and coconut flour along with baking soda, baking powder and cocoa powder.

4. Finally, press the batter into a lightly buttered cake pan. Air-fry for 35 minutes at 345 degrees F (174ºC).

5. In the meantime, make the frosting. Beat the butter and mascarpone cheese until creamy. Add in the melted chocolate chips and vanilla paste.

6. Gradually, stir in the Swerve and salt; beat until everything's well combined. Lastly, frost the brownies and serve

Nutrition: Calories: 363 Fat: 33g Protein: 7g Carbs: 10g Net carbs: 5gFiber: 5g

Butter Cake with Cranberries

Preparation time: 30 minutes

Cooking time: 20 minutes

Servings: 8

Ingredients:

- 1 cup almond flour
- $1/3$ teaspoon baking soda
- $1/3$ teaspoon baking powder
- ¾ cup erythritol
- ½ teaspoon ground cloves
- $1/3$ teaspoon ground cinnamon
- ½ teaspoon cardamom
- 1 stick butter
- ½ teaspoon vanilla paste
- 2 eggs plus 1 egg yolk, beaten
- ½ cup cranberries, fresh or thawed
- 1 tablespoon browned butter
- For Ricotta Frosting:
- ½ stick butter
- ½ cup firm Ricotta cheese
- 1 cup powdered erythritol
- ¼ teaspoon salt
- Zest of ½ lemon

Directions:

1. Start by preheating your Air Fryer to 355 degrees F (181ºC).

2. In a mixing bowl, combine the flour with baking soda, baking powder, erythritol, ground cloves, cinnamon, and cardamom.
3. In a separate bowl, whisk 1 stick butter with vanilla paste; mix in the eggs until light and fluffy. Add the flour/sugar mixture to the butter/egg mixture. Fold in the cranberries and browned butter.
4. Scrape the mixture into the greased cake pan. Then, bake in the preheated Air Fryer for about 20 minutes.
5. Meanwhile, in a food processor, whip ½ stick of the butter and Ricotta cheese until there are no lumps.
6. Slowly add the powdered erythritol and salt until your mixture has reached a thick consistency. Stir in the lemon zest; mix to combine and chill completely before using.
7. Frost the cake and enjoy!

Nutrition: Calories: 286 Fat: 27g Protein: 8g Carbs: 10g Net carbs: 5g Fiber: 5g

Buttery Monk Fruit Cookie

Preparation time: 25 minutes

Cooking time: 20 minutes

Servings: 4

Ingredients:

- 8 ounces (227 g) almond meal
- 2 tablespoons flaxseed meal
- 1 ounce (28 g) monk fruit
- 1 teaspoon baking powder
- A pinch of grated nutmeg
- A pinch of coarse salt
- 1 large egg, room temperature.
- 1 stick butter, room temperature
- 1 teaspoon vanilla extract

Directions:

1. Mix the almond meal, flaxseed meal, monk fruit, baking powder, grated nutmeg, and salt in a bowl.
2. In a separate bowl, whisk the egg, butter, and vanilla extract.
3. Stir the egg mixture into dry mixture; mix to combine well or until it forms a nice, soft dough.
4. Roll your dough out and cut out with a cookie cutter of your choice.

5. Bake in the preheated Air Fryer at 350 degrees F (180ºC) for 10 minutes. Decrease the temperature to 330 degrees F (166ºC) and cook for 10 minutes longer. Bon appétit!

Nutrition: Calories: 388 Fat: 38g Protein: 8g Carbs: 7g Net carbs: 4g Fiber: 3g

Buttery Cookie with Hazelnut

Preparation time: 20 minutes

Cooking time: 10 minutes

Servings: 6

Ingredients:

- 1 cup almond flour
- ½ cup coconut flour
- 1 teaspoon baking soda
- 1 teaspoon fine sea salt

- 1 stick butter
- 1 cup swerve
- 2 teaspoons vanilla
- 2 eggs, at room temperature
- 1 cup hazelnuts, coarsely chopped

Directions:

1. Begin by preheating your air fryer to 350 degrees f (180°c).
2. Mix the flour with the baking soda, and sea salt.
3. In the bowl of an electric mixer, beat the butter, swerve, and vanilla until creamy. Fold in the eggs, one at a time, and mix until well combined.
4. Slowly and gradually, stir in the flour mixture. Finally, fold in the coarsely chopped hazelnuts.
5. Divide the dough into small balls using a large cookie scoop; drop onto the prepared cookie sheets. Bake for 10 minutes or until golden brown, rotating the pan once or twice through the cooking time.
6. Work in batches and cool for a couple of minutes before removing to wire racks. Enjoy!

Nutrition: Calories: 328 Fat: 32g Protein: 7g Carbs: 5g Net carbs: 3g Fiber: 2g

CONCLUSION

Lip-smacking good, healthy and super simple, the Air Fryer Toast Oven will transform food in your home. With a complete guide on how it works, what to look out for and how to use to prepare different foods, you are now very well equipped to transform your kitchen!

With the tasty recipes included in this book, you may find yourself entertaining more than usual as everyone will want to come back for that unique taste that can only be delivered by an air fryer toast oven.

For the first time preparing these recipes, follow the instructions as is then with time feel free to add your special twist for a more personal touch.

While the very thought of preparing food in an air fryer toast oven may seem too complicated, you will be pleasantly surprised to learn that it's the easiest thing. The only thing required of you is to pay attention during the cooking process to avoid burning your food.

The greatest sell point of an air fryer toast oven is delicious meals with fewer calories compared to cooking the exact same meals the traditional way. An air fryer toast oven provides the best environment for bringing out the natural flavors of your ingredients.

Now, the only thing left is for you to get an air fryer toast oven that is going to suit your needs perfectly, if you don't already have one or if you need an upgrade. Remember to make healthy food choices for you to get the maximum low-calorie benefits. Occasionally you can treat yourself to some comfort food and your heart will thank you.

Enjoy the new way of life – cooking made easier and tastier!